River Thrill Sports

Superwheels & Thrill Sports

River Thrill Sports

ANDREW DAVID

TOM MORAN

Lerner Publications Company ▪ Minneapolis, Minnesota

ACKNOWLEDGMENTS: The photographs are reproduced through the courtesy of: pp. 6, 8, 10, 20, 30, 31, Stephen Titra; pp. 9, 16, 23, 38, 40, 46, Charles St. John; pp. 13, 14, 27, 32, 35, 43, Rob Lesser; p. 21, Richard Bangs; pp. 25, 26, H. Holmes; p. 37, Dave Shore; p. 18, Sobek Expeditions, Inc.

LIBRARY OF CONGRESS CATALOGING IN PUBLICATION DATA

River thrill sports.

(Superwheels & thrill sports)
Summary: A guide to the equipment, skills, and safety precautions required for rafting, canoeing, and kayaking. Also includes a glossary of pertinent terms and the international scale of river difficulty.
1. White-water canoeing—Juvenile literature. 2. Rafting (Sports)—Juvenile literature. [1. Rafting (Sports) 2. Canoes and canoeing. 3. White-water canoeing. 4. Kayaks and kayaking] I. Moran, Tom. II. Title. III. Series.
GV788.P34 1983   797.1'22   82-24966
ISBN 0-8225-0506-1 (lib. bdg.)

Manufactured in the United States of America

International Standard Book Number: 0-8225-0506-1
Library of Congress Catalog Card Number: 82-24966

1 2 3 4 5 6 7 8 9 10 90 89 88 87 86 85 84 83

CONTENTS

Canoes were among the first boats to navigate the rivers of the world. This modern canoe is a direct descendant of those early craft.

INTRODUCTION

For thousands of years, the earth's rivers have played a vital role in human life. Early people made crude rafts, log canoes, and woven reed boats to carry them over the water. Traveling on river currents, they crossed unknown mountain ranges and desert wastelands. The rivers became highways for commerce, transportation, and exploration, and great cities grew up on their banks.

With the development of modern trains, aircraft, and electronic communication, rivers became less important as channels of trade and information. But the world's waterways have continued to be a source of adventure for increasing numbers of boaters and rafters. River trips through lush marshlands or scenic forests offer a unique view of unspoiled natural settings, of wild animals and rare birds. For many boaters, however, the greatest river thrills come when the waters run fast and boil into a whitewater froth that tests a river runner's skill and daring.

The early river explorers did not share this fascination with the challenge of fast-running water. The steep cascades and high waves of rough water could easily capsize or sink their primitive boats. These were dangers to be avoided. When early travelers reached rapid-filled sections of rivers, they had to drag their boats ashore and *portage,* or carry, them overland until the river calmed enough to allow the voyage to continue safely.

The turbulent waves of whitewater rivers such as this present an exciting challenge to river runners.

Modern developments in boat design and materials have greatly reduced these dangers. Lightweight rafts and small boats are able to plunge over river waves and take on a deluge of water without sinking or capsizing. Boat hulls made of metal, fiberglass, and synthetic materials can be smashed against river boulders with little serious damage. These new kinds of river craft have turned once dangerous journeys into a thrilling sport—whitewater river running.

An inflatable raft is the newest kind of whitewater craft.

WHITEWATER CRAFT

Everything from inflated inner tubes to large commercial boats has been successfully used for river running, but the three most common river sport vessels are the canoe, the kayak, and the inflatable raft. Each is a descendent of early river craft, and each has its own unique history. All three vessels have special features that allow them to navigate the dangers of fast-flowing river waters. Let's take a look at these three kinds of whitewater craft.

The versatile canoe is equally at home on calm lakes and on fast-flowing rivers.

CANOES

The canoe was one of the first kinds of boats used by humans. Many primitive societies made crude dugout canoes by hollowing out tree trunks and logs. The American Indians developed more sophisticated wood-frame canoes that they covered with birchbark or animal hides. European explorers and fur trappers imitated the Indian designs, and their boats became important tools in the opening and development of the North American continent.

The narrow body and pointed ends of the traditional canoe give it both high speed and maneuverability. These features make the canoe ideal for weaving through obstacles like rocks and fallen trees and around tricky bends in a fast-moving river. Most canoes have plenty of space for stowing large amounts of camping gear and supplies. Because of this, they are excellent for use on extended wilderness trips.

Modern developments in materials and design have increased the canoe's ability to withstand the stresses of river running. Aluminum, fiberglass, and plastic canoes are now commonly used in whitewater conditions. All are lightweight, durable, and, with some exceptions, easy to repair. The choice of a canoe material and style depends on the river use the craft will receive and how much a canoeist can afford to pay. Personal preference is also a factor in making this important choice.

Canoe paddles are usually made of spruce, ash, or some other durable wood. Some whitewater canoeists prefer paddles made of fiberglass, plastic, or aluminum. Others like to use long wooden or metal poles to guide and propel their canoes in relatively calm water.

Special *decked canoes* are made for use in severe whitewater conditions and in river competitions. The deck encloses the canoe and prevents water from splashing in and slowing or sinking it. The paddler kneels inside a small open cockpit with special braces to help him or her stay in position.

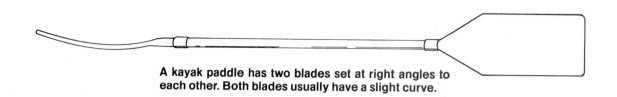

A kayak paddle has two blades set at right angles to each other. Both blades usually have a slight curve.

KAYAKS

A kayak (KI-ak) is another kind of boat specially designed to keep out water. Kayaks were originally developed by Eskimos for use in the frigid waters of the Arctic Ocean. The early models were made of wooden frames covered with stretched sealskins. They were easily maneuverable and capable of threading through the icebergs and floes that fill the northern waters.

Most importantly, the Eskimo kayak was a closed boat. The animal-skin covering enclosed all but a small cockpit where the paddler sat, sealed into the boat by a heavy fur parka. The icy waters were unable to penetrate the Eskimo kayak, even if it accidently rolled over.

Modern adaptations of these features have made the kayak popular for whitewater recre-

ation. Sleek kayaks are now made of fiberglass or synthetic materials such as polyethylene. The paddler sits in the small cockpit area of the kayak, held in position by foot, thigh, and knee braces. A waterproof *spray skirt* seals the paddler inside the boat and keeps river water and spray from pouring aboard.

A kayak is propelled by a long double-ended paddle. When one blade of the paddle is in the water pushing the boat forward, the other blade is moving through the air and into position for a stroke on the opposite side of the kayak. Modern kayak paddles have the blades set at right angles to each other. This means that when a blade is out of the water, its narrow edge cuts through the air, reducing wind resistance. The blades of early Eskimo paddles were not set at right angles, and paddling with them required much more effort.

As one blade of a kayak paddle flashes through the air, the other blade pushes the kayak through the water.

About to capsize, this kayaker has begun a maneuver called the Eskimo roll, which will turn the craft upright again.

When performing an Eskimo roll, a kayaker holds the paddle parallel to the side of the kayak as the boat begins to capsize (1 and 2). Underwater, the kayaker sweeps the paddle into a vertical position (3). This motion, combined with a twist of the kayaker's body, will roll the kayak over and bring the kayaker out of the water (4 and 5).

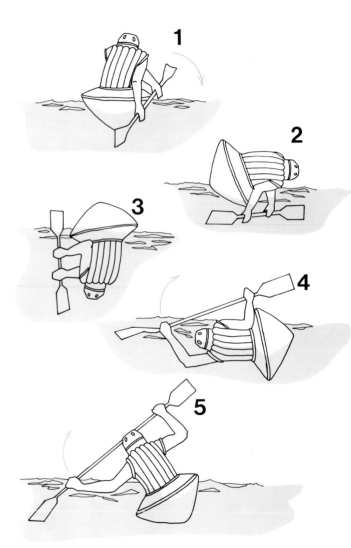

Because of its design and construction, a modern kayak is extremely buoyant and can be quickly and easily turned. The craft's sealed deck allows it to plunge through waves and under cascades that would sink an open canoe. A kayak does have some disadvantages when compared to a canoe. The paddler sits lower than a canoeist and does not have as much visibility. Kayaks also have much less space for storing gear and supplies than canoes.

One of the most important features of a kayak is that it is almost impossible to sink. If strong currents or river waves flip it over, the kayak will remain afloat. The paddler can use the river current, the paddle, and his or her body weight to flip the boat upright again with a quick rolling motion. This maneuver is called the *Eskimo roll* and is learned by all kayakers before they venture out on a river run.

A set of long wooden oars guides this raft through the turbulent water.

INFLATABLE RAFTS

Inflatable rafts are the newest vessels used for wildwater river running. They are descendents of the life rafts developed for sea rescue during World War II. Because of the increased popularity of commercial raft trips, rafting is probably the easiest way for a beginner to try out river running.

Rafts come in a variety of styles that range from 9-foot-long inflatables with room for two people to 36-foot-long *pontoon boats* that can hold many passengers and their equipment. The body of a raft is made of puncture-resistant material and composed of many small *flotation chambers,* individual air compartments that are linked together. If one chamber is damaged and loses air, the remaining flotation chambers will keep the raft buoyant.

Most rafts are fitted with wood or metal rowing frames so that a set of oars may be used to control the craft's progress. Some rafts are maneuvered by two or more paddles, depending on the size of the vessel. The use of paddles allows more passengers to participate in the river trip action, but oars give much better control over a raft.

Inflatable rafts have tremendous buoyancy. Because they glide over the top of the water rather than through it, they are able to bounce off huge boulders and bound through giant waves that would demolish other kinds of boats. With a skilled person at the oars, rafts can navigate the most ferocious whitewater.

Constructed of many small flotation chambers, an inflatable raft is so buoyant that it can bound through high waves without capsizing.

Most rafters are introduced to wildwater on commercial float trips. On these trips, a professional rafter acts as a pilot, taking a group of people on a river journey lasting a day or more. Passengers on a float trip often take a turn at the oars or shift their weight at the guide's command. Float trips can be exciting educations in river adventure, giving beginners a chance to learn about the river and the ways of approaching its hazards.

SAFETY

Although modern materials and boat designs have reduced many of river running's hazards, it is still a dangerous recreation. Each year whitewater enthusiasts are injured because they were careless or unprepared or because they underestimated the danger that they faced. Preparation and a concern for safety will greatly reduce the risks of a wild river trip.

No one should start out on a river trip without the skills necessary to complete it. Knowing how to paddle a canoe or kayak across a calm, flat lake does not mean that you have the skill to confront torrents of river wildwater in the same vessel. River runners must be able not only to handle their craft but also to deal with the river conditions they will face.

Basic paddling or rowing techniques should be practiced on calm water and then tested on sections of rough water where mistakes will not mean disaster. To choose a spot for a test of skills, beginners should consult guidebooks that use the International Scale of River Difficulty. This rating system, in use all over the world, grades rivers on a scale that ranges from Class I (mild water) to Class VI (very dangerous and nearly impossible), based on the existence of rapids, waves, and other hazards. Once Class I rivers have been mastered, progressively more difficult river sections may be attempted.

One easy way for beginners to get started in river running is by taking a class. Organized classes are available in basic kayak and canoe skills as well as in moving water techniques. They are often sponsored by local YMCAs and YWCAs, Red Cross branches, and wilderness outfitters.

River runners must be able to handle their craft on calm water before facing the challenge of a wild river.

No matter how much experience they have, river runners can find themselves in trouble on a whitewater trip. A single mistake in judgment and they are swimming in the river, their boat damaged, sunk, or hurtling downstream without them. It is this possibility, for beginner and expert alike, that makes safety equipment necessary on all river running trips.

Some pieces of equipment are essential to protect the river runner's personal safety. Buoyant life preservers or jackets keep a canoeist, kayaker, or rafter afloat in the water. Padded helmets protect the river runner's head from collisions with rocks or submerged logs. Tennis or running shoes protect the feet from the same dangers and come in very handy if an accident forces a river runner to walk along the shore in search of assistance.

A life jacket and padded helmet are important pieces of safety equipment for kayakers and other river runners.

Even on a warm spring or summer day, many rivers are icy cold, often filled with melted snow running off from the mountains upstream. A canoeist, kayaker, or rafter suddenly thrown into these chilly waters risks *hypothermia,* a subnormal body temperature caused by immersion in cold water. This condition increases physical exhaustion and greatly reduces the river runner's chances of survival. A rubber *wet suit* keeps the body temperature up in cold water and helps to prevent hypothermia. Wet suits should be worn on any river trip where the water temperature might drop below 50 degrees Fahrenheit (10 degrees Centigrade).

Some kinds of safety equipment are needed to keep a river runner's craft in good condition. Rafts and canoes should be equipped with buckets or plastic containers for bailing out water from inside the boat. Safety line for use in rescue or for guiding boats down especially dangerous river sections is important cargo on whitewater trips. Many canoeists and kayakers also carry extra flotation devices such as pieces of foam, which help keep their boats afloat in a river spill. Emergency rations and a boat repair kit are needed in case a river runner should become stranded miles from aid.

Trip planning is as important as safety equipment. Before departing, river runners should let friends know their route, destination, and expected arrival time so that a search can be made if they do not arrive on schedule. Of course, river trips should never be attempted alone. These are simple precautions that can insure a safe and enjoyable river adventure.

Scouting a river from shore prepares river runners for the hazards they will face.

READING THE RIVER

The key to success in any river trip is understanding the hazards ahead and then choosing a route downriver that avoids or reduces potential dangers. A fast-moving river can be "read" like a map. Experienced river runners scout each river section from shore before venturing forward on their trip. From the river banks, their sharp eyes scan the rough water, spotting sunken boulders or hidden obstacles and locating the course options available to them. Before entering their boats, the river runners have mentally charted the route they will take, one that will give them an exciting but controlled ride through the rapids below.

It takes experience to correctly read and understand a fast-moving river. Each river is different, but numerous common features will reappear in the tell-tale whitewater patterns. Seasoned river runners are able to spot *tongues,* wide V-patterns pointing *downstream* (in the direction of the river current), which will lead them between rocks. On the downstream side of rock formations and other obstructions, they will look for *eddies,* pools of calm water in the midst of raging streams. V-patterns pointing *upstream* will indicate the location of submerged rocks and boulders. A long, unbroken horizontal line warns them of dams or severe vertical drops that must be avoided.

River runners also keep a sharp eye out for *chutes* or *jets,* fast-moving, turbulent channels between rocks or river banks. At the bottom of these passages, they can expect to find lines of *standing waves* that must be crossed to continue downstream. These waves are formed when fast water rushes into sections of slower water. When the waves get very large, as they do at the end of a long steep chute, they are called *haystacks.*

Suckholes are another common river hazard. They are found when water flows over rocks or other obstacles with so much force that its flow is reversed at the base of the obstacle. The currents of water moving in opposite directions form a hole that can trap a boat in its center, making it difficult to move upstream or downstream. Other names for these dangerous water traps are *souseholes, keepers,* or *reversals.*

No matter how experienced they become, river runners never tackle a new river without thoroughly scouting its hazards. They also consult guidebooks, U.S. Geological Survey maps, local wilderness outfitters, and government rangers for additional information on the river and any special hazards they might face. When the studying and scouting are done, the downriver adventure begins.

These rafters are looking for a tongue, a V-shaped pattern in the water that will lead them to a safe route through the rapids ahead.

Its bow submerged in the water, a raft plunges down a fast-moving chute.

A kayaker caught in the surging water of a suckhole formed at the base of a drop

CANOEING THE RAPIDS

Navigating rapids in an open canoe is one of river running's most challenging thrills. With two people paddling, it is an exercise in teamwork, concentration, and skill. Their slender craft gripped by the river's power, the paddlers must fight for control to achieve a safe, exhilarating river run.

Let's follow two canoeists as they begin a run. With the scouting complete and a plan of attack decided upon, the canoe team heads for the rapids. The river's current is strong, and there is little need for forward paddling as the canoe is carried toward a "rock garden" (a cluster of rocks) boiling with whitewater.

The paddles dip into the water to position the boat between two rocks that signal the first chute. The current speeds up, and the water deepens as the front end, or *bow,* of the canoe plunges into the downward flowing water. Rocks slip by in a blur, and the sound of the river becomes a low roar. From inside the speeding canoe, the paddlers have a very different view than they did when they were scouting the river from shore.

The paddlers dig their paddles into the water again, trying to position the canoe so that its bow makes a slight angle when it smacks into the standing waves at the chute's bottom. As they hit the waves, spray flies and water splashes into the canoe. The paddlers fight to keep cross currents from upsetting their boat, using their paddles in a *brace* stroke to maintain their balance and to stay on course.

A stretch of rough water ahead promises an exciting ride for a team of canoeists.

The canoeists enter a section of rapids strewn with rocks and boulders.

The canoeists are committed and there is no turning back now that they are in the rapids. Their canoe rushes forward, snaking through the rocks and finding chute after chute with its sharp bow. Finally they drive into a long steep chute between two large rocks and spurt forward suddenly. At the bottom, a high wave—a haystack—is waiting for them.

With their paddles straining against the water, the canoeists work to spin the canoe so that it will hit the haystack almost broadside. The boat crunches into the wall of water, hangs for a minute amid a shower of spray, and then bounds forward. The river runners have arrived in calm water, and the first set of rapids is behind them. They laugh together as they bail out the water that has poured into their boat. The canoeists take a final look at the stretch of water they have just mastered and then begin to paddle forward into the current, eager to tackle the next set of rapids.

Maneuvering through choppy waves, the canoe team heads for a patch of calm water.

This kayaker is almost hidden
by the foaming water of a jet.

KAYAKING IN WHITEWATER

River runners who choose kayaks can handle fiercer whitewater than those with canoes. One-person kayaks are the most popular type used for river running. Often groups of a half dozen kayaks will head downriver in "follow-the-leader" style. The kayakers call and signal to one another as they progress around bends and down steep, rocky stretches of rapids.

The lead kayak moves out first, its long paddle flashing like a hummingbird's wings as it drives for the first downstream jet. The kayaker is sitting close to the water in her small boat, and the river seems to be rushing by at breakneck speed. From this low vantage point, small waves look gigantic as the kayak darts through small canyons formed by rock and boulder formations. It is a tricky course, and each chute brings the small craft closer to loss of control.

After a few minutes of frantic action, the kayaker slips down alongside a large boulder and leans over to drive one end of the paddle into the water. This maneuver pivots the boat into the calm water of an eddy formed behind the boulder. From this protected spot, the kayaker pauses briefly to survey the water ahead and choose the best route. Confident, she peels off into the fast-moving stream again, letting her body weight and the strong currents turn the nimble kayak.

The opposing currents of water in a suckhole can trap a boat and prevent it from moving forward.

The little vessel moves quickly downstream, hopping from eddy to eddy under complete control. But now the kayaker sees a suckhole ahead, formed where water is cascading over the top of a submerged rock ledge. Large suckholes are dangerous, but this one is small enough that the experienced kayaker can attempt it. She dips the paddle blades several times, pulling against the stream to slow the kayak's descent. The boat slips over the ledge and its sharp nose plummets into the turbulent

hole. The river's forces toss the kayak around like an amusement park ride, spinning it diagonally with each surge of the water.

To work her way out of the water hole's grip, the kayaker braces downstream and then paddles forward. A few deft strokes and the kayak is parked within the safety of another eddy. Satisfied with her efforts, the paddler looks back upstream to see how her companions will make it through the surging waters of the suckhole.

Its stern pointing to the sky, a kayak plunges over a steep drop.

RAFTING THE BIG ONES

Inflatable river rafts can navigate torrents of water that would spell certain doom for kayaks and canoes. But even raft trips must be undertaken with caution and planning. If they aren't, the large inflatables could end up pinned helplessly against a rock outcropping or flipped upside down by the savage river forces.

Even commercial raft trips that are run frequently over the same stretch of river can face unexpected trouble. Each trip is a little different because of changes in weather and river flows and because of the split-second timing required to get through tricky whitewater sections. A professional river guide must use all of his or her skill to get each party of passengers safely to the end of their adventure.

The adventure begins when one of the big rafts approaches the first stretch of rapids. The passengers recheck their life jackets as the sound of the turbulent water becomes a loud warning roar. Pulling on the oars, the guide propels the raft into the first chute of water racing downstream. The current grabs the buoyant inflatable, and it shoots forward like a rocket, only to be slammed into a wave at the bottom of the drop. Water pours into the raft, drenching the passengers. They tighten their grips on the safety lines and try to peer through the frothy water ahead.

One rafter handles the oars while another keeps a sharp eye out for submerged logs and other obstacles.

Heading for a drop, a rafter pulls up the bow of the raft to keep it from diving under the water.

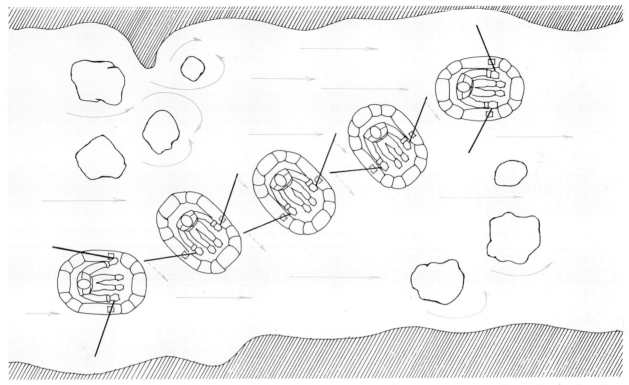

In ferrying, the stern of the raft is pointed in the direction that the rafter wants to move. The rafter pushes the oars forward through the water to move the raft across the current at an angle.

At the bottom of the second long chute, the raft folds nearly in half from the impact of another wave. It plummets forward, bouncing off rocks like a pinball and rolling almost on end. Now the guide pulls hard on the thick wooden oars, trying to *ferry*, or cut across the current at an angle in order to avoid a gaping suckhole that might trap the raft.

Water sprays high as a raft crashes into a standing wave.

The inflatable boat, heavy with the water it has taken in, slides past the edge of the foaming hole and heads into the final chute. It crashes into the waiting wave with a thudding sound, and a curtain of water showers aboard.

As the raft breaks free into the calm water below, the drenched passengers shout in exhilaration. The pilot releases his oars and breathes a sigh of relief. Everyone on board will remember these wildwater thrills for a long time.

WHITEWATER COMPETITION

River running is not only a popular recreation but also an exciting competitive sport. Every year the popularity of whitewater competition increases throughout the world. Races are held for both kayaks and closed-deck canoes under the sponsorship of organizations such as the International Canoe Federation, the American Canoe Association, and the American Whitewater Affiliation. Competitors are usually divided into classes depending on their age, sex, and abilities.

The two most popular types of races are *slalom* and *wildwater* competitions. Both are conducted under strict supervision on fast-moving rivers or specially constructed artificial courses. They give competitors a chance to test their skills against both the whitewater and their fellow paddlers.

Slalom races are run over short stretches of river that have been marked with sets of poles suspended on lines over the water. The sets of poles, or gates, form a winding downstream course. Each canoeist or kayaker must travel the course as quickly as possible, controlling his or her boat so that it passes through each gate in the proper order. If a gate is missed or if the boat touches one of the poles, the competitor is given a penalty of additional seconds that are added to the elapsed time for the course. The winner is the person who gets through the course in the shortest amount of time.

In a slalom race, a kayaker or canoeist must maneuver through a series of gates suspended over the water of a fast-moving river.

No gates are used in wildwater racing. These races are usually run over longer courses than are slalom competitions. The object is to go downriver as rapidly as possible without spilling or getting trapped in the turbulent waters. Many racers will be on the course at the same time, and the faster boats must pass their slower competition. To get the most speed, the racers propel themselves downstream on the very edge of control.

Both slalom and wildwater races attract numerous competitors and spectators. They provide great opportunities to watch and learn from the top river runners as they take on whitewater's most challenging tests.

A kayak's sharp bow cuts through a wall of sparkling foam. Only the most experienced river runners can handle wildwater this fierce.

GLOSSARY

blade—The broad, flattened part of an oar or paddle

bow (BAU)—The front end of a boat

brace—A paddle stroke in which the blade is braced or pushed against the water; used to maintain or restore balance

channel—The main bed and deepest part of a river

chute—A narrow passage where the water flows faster than in the rest of the river

decked canoe—A whitewater canoe with a deck covering its top portion

downstream—In the direction that the river current flows

drop—A place where a river suddenly descends

eddy—An area of calm water formed behind obstructions

Eskimo roll—A technique for righting a capsized kayak

ferry—To paddle a boat at an angle across the current

flotation—Pieces of foam or inflatable air bags added to a canoe or kayak to increase its buoyancy

flotation chambers—Self-contained inflatable compartments that make up a raft

haystack—A large standing wave

hull—The frame or body of a boat

hypothermia (hi-po-THER-mee-uh)—A subnormal body temperature caused by immersion in cold water

jet—Another word for a chute

pontoon boat—A large inflatable raft made of long cylinder-shaped sections or pontoons *portage*—To carry a boat overland from one body of water to another or from one part of a river to another in order to avoid an impassable area

put-in—The place where a river trip begins; also the action of putting a boat in the water

rapids—A section of a river with turbulent water, usually with obstacles and waves

rowing frame—A wood or metal structure set on top of an inflatable raft so that it may be controlled with oars

slalom (SLAHL-uhm) race—A river race in which each boat must pass through a series of course markers or gates

spray skirt—A flexible waterproof sheet that fits over a kayaker's lower body and keeps water from splashing inside the boat

standing wave—A river wave formed when fast-moving water flows into a body of slower water

stern—The rear end of a boat

suckhole—An area in which water flows over an obstacle with such force that the direction of the river current is reversed

take-out—The place where a river trip ends; also the action of taking a boat out of the water

tongue—A V-shaped area of fast water at the head of rapids

trough—A depression between waves

upstream—In the direction opposite to the river's current

wet suit—A suit of rubberized clothing designed to maintain a person's body temperature in cold water

whitewater—Rapids characterized by turbulent, foamy water

wildwater race—A river race in which competitors choose their own course downstream

THE INTERNATIONAL SCALE OF RIVER DIFFICULTY

Rapids on a river generally fit into one of the following classifications. If the water temperature is below 50 degrees Fahrenheit, however, a river section would be considered one class more difficult than normal. The river's difficulty might also be increased if the whitewater trip planned is a long one in a wilderness area.

Class I:
Moving water with a few riffles and small waves; few or no obstructions.

Class II:
Easy rapids with waves up to three feet high; wide, clearly visible channels that require some maneuvering.

Class III:
Rapids with high irregular waves, often capable of swamping an open canoe; narrow passages that may require complex maneuvering.

Class IV:
Long, difficult rapids with constricted passages that often require precise maneuvering in very turbulent waters; generally not possible for open canoes; boaters in covered canoes and kayaks should be able to Eskimo roll, rescue is difficult.

Class V:
Extremely difficult; long and very violent rapids with heavily congested routes; rescue conditions difficult; significant hazard to life in event of a mishap; ability to Eskimo roll essential.

Class VI:
Difficulties of Class V carried to the extreme of navigability; nearly impossible and very dangerous; for teams of experts only after close study and with all precautions taken.

Superwheels & Thrill Sports

Lerner Publications Company
241 First Avenue North, Minneapolis, Minnesota 55401